# Italy: Lost in Seeing

# Italy: Lost in Seeing

Photographs by *Mimmo Jodice*

with 193 illustrations, 172 in duotone

 Thames & Hudson

'A Biographical Account' translated from the Italian 'Racconto biografico' by Clare Costa

First published in the United Kingdom in 2007 by Thames & Hudson Ltd, 181A High
Holborn, London WC1V 7QX

www.thamesandhudson.com

British Library Cataloguing-in-Publication Data
A catalogue record for this book is available from the British Library

ISBN 978-0-500-54355-9

Printed in Italy

# Contents

# The Power of Images

## Francine Prose

It's difficult, maybe impossible, to say even one true thing about a country, or about the people who live there. Every adjective suggests its opposite. Every statement evokes the contradiction that leads, in turn, to the paradox. Even the smallest country is large. A country is as rich as its wealthiest inhabitant and as poor as its most indigent citizen. The progressive and the reactionary, the innovative and the traditional co-exist within the same region, the same neighbourhood, on the same block. The lacy towers of the cathedral may rise from the midst of the grittiest urban slum, just as the newly excavated foundation of the yet-to-be-built skyscraper may turn out to contain the ruins of an ancient civilization.

Given the challenge of conveying anything useful or accurate about a characteristic landscape or cityscape, a culture or a national character – and assuming there *is* such a thing as a national character – it's no wonder that we so often succumb to the temptation of the stereotype and cliché. Everyone knows that the cowboy hat and polyester shorts are the basics of the American wardrobe, just as the popular imagination stubbornly insists on the cartoon of the Frenchman in a beret and stripy shirt. And Italy? There's the Colosseum, the singing gondolier, and Mamma in a long black dress with a colossal bowl of pasta, of course! Meanwhile, history has shown us, again and again, that the reductive is not only unhelpful but dangerous in its ability to foster a blindness that obscures the complexity, the beauty and the humanity of anything or anyone that seems unfamiliar, or foreign.

Mimmo Jodice's haunting and evocative photographs, collected together in this book, subvert all the readily available and useless clichés of national identity. They make us realize that the stereotypical and the reductive create, and then proceed to exist in, a kind of bogus eternity, in which a place or a people can always be depended on to look, and behave in, more or less the same way.

In fact, these pictures compel us to reconsider the meaning of – and our relationship with – time itself, and, by extension, eternity. In several of these photos, the ruin and the construction site seem nearly indistinguishable, as if they are somehow meeting halfway along the continuum that links the past with the future. We all know that the snapping of a photograph transpires within a single instant. But *which* instant, precisely, have these images been taken in? In their uncanny ability to telescope and lengthen time, to compress and expand the moment, to blur the line between present and past, between the contemporary and the historical, these photographs suggest the wonders that might have been produced if Proust had been enticed to leave his cork-lined bedroom, given a camera, and encouraged to spend decades travelling in, and photographing, Italy.

Jodice's work not only challenges our unexamined assumptions about how a country (in this case, Italy) looks, but also causes us to recalculate the old formulation of the numerical relationship between the image and the word: the notion that a single one of the former is 'worth' a thousand of the latter. These photos – the visual record of a thirty-year odyssey around the artist's native land – remind us of the power of the image to represent something that strikes us immediately as true, as informative and revealing, but for which there *are* no words, a truth for which no words exist. They confirm our sense that, in the realm of art, subject matter is always and only the humble servant of vision. Jodice takes pictures of sites that every traveller visits, or those that even the most visually astute and conscious citizen might pass right by without noticing, and he sees them (and allows us to see them) in an entirely different way, a way that, we feel, no one else ever has, or ever will.

To describe Jodice's photographs is a bit like trying to summarize the theme or the narrative of a poem, and coming to understand, once again, that the beauty of poetry resides in what cannot be reduced or translated into anything but itself. These images are at once seriously and joyously formal. They are formal in the simplest sense. That is, they call our attention to geometry and shape; they remind us of the glories of the arch, the stubborn intransigence of the rectangle, the goofy spires and creases of a folded beach umbrella. Yet one of the most striking things about them is how some mysterious aspect of lighting or composition – or again, let's say, of art – so offhandedly burns away the chill of the formal, the glacial petrified beauty of a Mapplethorpe or Weston. These pictures suggest something original about the possibilities of form. Could it be that the most interesting formalism might be a little... messy? Like those of the Surrealists, Jodice's lens peers through webs of fencing and through the rents in scrims of diaphanous fabric, and makes the detritus of modern life seem like the height of wit and the very apex of high design. They make us look twice, and then again at something we might never have noticed: cars parked and covered by their protective shrouds in a plaza in Naples, the tracery of leafless vines on a wall in Milan or San Marino.

How oddly *populated* these photos seem, though the humans in them are more likely to decorate the walls of Pompeii and the pillars of a subterranean chapel than crowd a city street or gather in any of the spots where we are more accustomed to finding our fellow creatures. Often, Jodice invites us into rooms, or urban spaces, or landscapes whose inhabitants appear to have departed suddenly or unexpectedly, though again we cannot hope to say when everyone left. Was it a moment, or a century, or a thousand years in the past? Everywhere, we confront the contrast between the ornate and the spare, the blank wall and the mural, the starkly plain and the overdecorated, and we're invited to ponder the implications and the meaning of those departures, of those absences and of that busy, nattering detail. Consider the images of the San Sabba memorial, Trieste – a tribute to the victims who passed through the former rice factory when it was converted to a deportation centre for Italian Jews in the Second World War. Jodice's deceptively effortless pictures inspire us to think about how hard it is to render emptiness in art, and what an achievement it is to make those bare walls as eloquent and powerfully claustrophobic in two dimensions as they are in three.

Indeed, we can hardly imagine a more animated set of landscapes and cityscapes, of still lifes that seem anything but still. The statues of the athletes from Herculaneum strike us as being just on the point of sprinting away, and the ancient sculptures appear to be yearning. How much they would like to say to us, if only they could! In Jodice's work, even the plants and stones – the writhing agave, the roots of a banyan tree in Syracuse, the bare branches hanging along the banks of the Tiber, the paving stones along a road in Calabria – seem to have been momentarily arrested in the midst of constant motion. The natural and the manmade interact in ways that make it seem as if man and nature are co-designers working together to produce panoramas of hybrid beauty.

As difficult as it is to make a statement about a country or a people, it is even harder to talk about a dream. Every writer knows that only the greatest geniuses (Tolstoy, for example) can take the risk of using a dream in fiction, for fear that the reader's attention will wander just as it does when our dearest friends and loved ones tell us, over breakfast, about the phantasms that visited them during the night. And yet it is impossible not to talk about the dreamlike quality of Mimmo Jodice's photographs. They possess the sly wit, the odd logic, and the absolute persuasiveness of the images that our unconscious generates to alarm or entertain us as we sleep.

Which brings me to what may be the most remarkable thing of all: the way in which art can make a dream seem more 'real' than the visible world that we ourselves have observed. We think of photos as capturing and rendering reality, but rarely of photos replacing it. And yet...no matter how often I visit Paris, it always seems less tangible and convincing to me – certainly less memorable – than the Atget images that have, for so long, taken up residence in my imagination.

The images in this book enable us to see Italy as it really is, as it exists and persists in our dreams, and in an entirely fresh and unique way. Once having seen these marvellous works, we can no longer encounter the Italian landscape without realizing that a country we may assume we know has a secret identity, and that Italy is, after all, a series of Mimmo Jodice photographs.

# Dreams and Visions of Italy

## Alessandra Mauro

This book brings together a selection of photographs dedicated to Italy – unique images and personal visions collected by Mimmo Jodice over the course of thirty years of life and work, image after image, vision after vision. Throughout this period Jodice has been a prolific photographer of Italy; and he has travelled its length and breadth, from the peaks of the Alps to the tip of Sicily, capturing large cities and small villages as well as rural landscapes, forgotten corners and renowned monuments, disused factories and town squares. He has done this as a profession and a craft, undoubtedly, but he has also been driven by an unremitting desire to explore and discover the motivation behind his life as an artist and interpreter of places, of human traces, of nature, of ancient history, of a complex and contradictory present. It is as if, on picking up the camera, he felt compelled to find just the right viewpoint and the right moment (which are different every time) to record and interpret the nature of the precarious balance between space and mankind. The endless desire to see, the freedom to lose himself not only in whatever lies before his eyes but also in the meandering paths of memory: these are the things that form the fabric of these visual journeys; following many roads, some quite unfamiliar, they build up a multifaceted image of an Italy that immediately becomes a universal territory.

Jodice discovered photography at an early age, and his interest soon grew into a wish to study, experiment and explore. He lived through the years of conceptual experimentation of the 1960s, and immediately set about searching for new languages and new codes with which to express himself. The earliest images in this book date from the 1970s, from the era of his so-called 'social' photography, in which Jodice created work that was rooted in the social fabric of his city and its avant-garde.

Right from the start he sought questions rather than answers, trying to go beyond mere documentary work to deliver a personal account, a concept that would reach maturity in the 1980s and 1990s. The major book *Vedute di Napoli* came out in 1980, and depicts Naples as a city which is densely populated and crowded with figures and reference points, full of voices, of dramas played out and interpreted, and with its *dramatis personae* intent on performing their own roles; and yet its noisy nature is suppressed. The scenes unfold in silence and the photographs become metaphysical visions of a place where Jodice's doubts and fears gather and take shape. Traces of the past come to infiltrate the present, bringing it to life and tormenting it with its terrifying power. It was this personal approach, so far removed from a simple journalistic account, that went on to become Jodice's instantly recognizable style.

Within the context of contemporary art of the same period and an ongoing debate with fellow photographers and artists about the theme of place, Jodice's long examination of Italy's artistic heritage drove him to focus more closely on meaning and the value of spatial representation. He actively sought and pursued beauty, but found it in archaeological fragments or in the purity of nature; it is captured by Jodice's lens with the melancholic certainty of a man who is well aware that just beyond the vision of perfection, the play of lights which exalt and enliven a classicism that seemed long since gone, there lies an invasive and infectious chaos that could sweep everything away in a whirl of oblivion. His photography becomes an act of exposure, of rebellion, proof of a clear and tangible unease, hitting the nerves of a city rich in opportunities but also plagued by troubles and traumas; it becomes a necessary reversal of meaning, on the border between a present that seeks verification and a past that needs to be questioned.

After the images of Naples come other cities, other visions. And increasingly it is silence that becomes the dominant element. A silence full of voices whose chatter has come to an abrupt stop, of footsteps that have ceased to echo. A silence that understands history, and the paradox of using a photograph to capture something that cannot be seen. Who has lived in the places that Jodice photographs for us? Who has constructed them from layer upon layer of stones and passing time? His work becomes the photography of non-existence.

But Jodice does not create photographs of memory; on the contrary, he photographs the present. And the spaces he moves through are his own, part of the here and now, filled with the real fears of a contemporary artist who is searching for meaning in his own life and in the images he creates. If we use a theatrical metaphor to describe Jodice's photography – a stage on which the performance has just begun – we can extend this into a new image: the 15th-century concept of the 'theatre of memory', an imaginary location in which the eyes of the spectator/creator can shape and rearrange the elements of the set, and then place within this setting some sequence of objects that the memory wishes to store – an arrangement dictated by personal choice, but which is necessary if the name, function and significance of the objects is to be correctly recalled. It is these things, the name, function and significance of the objects – be they statues, faces, landscapes, trees, beaches, factories, almost all traces of human life – that Jodice constantly recalls, rearranges, alters and rebuilds in each new setting, giving it a meaning that is quite different from the one we would normally apply. An alienating meaning, which suggests that perceived reality and vision do not always agree.

This book thus brings together the different stages – like a sequence of stopping points – of Jodice's long journey up and down Italy in a quest for new ways of seeing. And this was how the book came about, from an awareness that this body of work has great strength, coherence and unity. It is as if Jodice stopped suddenly in his tracks, gripped by a desire to turn back, having grasped the significance of so much travelling across Italy during his many years as a photographer; it is as if, in that moment, he understood that they constituted his own personal tale of the *viaggiatore eccellente* who can read the deep and intimate poetry of a country which is so often hidden from the eyes of an observer.

The simplicity of monochrome, the extraordinary sharpness of the images, an ability to surprise and stop you in your tracks as your eyes come to rest on moments and situations that might have seemed surreal had they not been clues to that new code of meaning which Jodice presents to us like a key to power, so that we too can learn to re-examine our own surroundings with fresh eyes.

Each image thus becomes both a personal vision and a view, in the sense of understanding a detailed representation of a place, whether shaped by man or nature. And if reality and vision do not always coincide, perhaps the dream and the vision will – the dream of an Italy that seems somehow different, an Italy to fall hopelessly in love with, an Italy that is endlessly engaging and impossible to forget.

Dreams became the guiding metaphor for this book, giving Mimmo Jodice's images their basic sequence. Six different paths bring together images, glimpses and landscapes, which are united by a continuous thread of cross-references and details like links in a chain, creating new contours. The paths are not geographical in nature but reflections of the mind, of sight, of memory, of free associations that carry us from Naples to the Via Emilia, to Biella and then back to Naples again. Each one of these 'dreams of dreams' starts with an opening image: a doorway that allows us access to the magical vision of this beautiful and fragile Italy, and to the relics of a past that still remains, forming the backbone of our present.

It is Jodice's visionary skill, ancient and lyrical, which makes his artistic path during these years so unique – crystal-clear and utterly original. The powerful importance he attaches to testimony, to the interpretation of a living past, to the continual questioning of the complex present and a future that possesses the urgent, almost visceral need for an artistic act to affirm its own existence.

'And what of the value of dreams in regard to our knowledge of the future? That, of course, is quite out of the question. One would like to substitute the words: in regard to our knowledge of the past. For in every sense a dream has its origin in the past. The ancient belief that dreams reveal the future is not indeed entirely devoid of the truth. By representing a wish as fulfilled the dream certainly leads us into the future; but this future, which the dreamer accepts as his present, has been shaped in the likeness of the past by the indestructible wish.'

Sigmund Freud, *The Interpretation of Dreams*

I'd like to begin by quoting Fernando Pessoa: '…but what was I thinking about before I got lost in seeing?' This phrase seems to be written for me, and describes my recurring behaviour quite well: I lose myself in seeing, imagining, and following visions outside reality.

*Città Visibili/Visible Cities*, Milan: Charta, 2006

Naples, 1999. Real Albergo dei Poveri.

Capua, 1993. Amphitheatre.

Milan, 2003. Spazio Erasmus.

Rome, 1996.

Rome, 2005. San Carlo alle Quattro Fontane.

Agrigento, 1993. Temple of Concord.

Baia, 1986. Castle.

Bitonto, 1998. Cathedral.

Teramo, 2000. Archaeological Museum.

Naples, 1980. Centro Antico.

Milan, 2000. Chiaravalle Abbey.

Naples, 1987. Suor Orsola.

Rome, 1999. St Peter's Square.

Pozzuoli, 1993. Flavian amphitheatre.

Riva del Garda, 2007. Hospital.

Turin, 2005. Le Nuove prison.

Naples, 1987. Suor Orsola.

Capri, 1984. Villa Sarah.

Via Emilia, 1985.

Biella, 2007. Oasi Zegna park.

Pompeii, 1982. Basilica.

Naples, 1987. Real Albergo dei Poveri.

Naples, 1990. Castel Sant'Elmo.

I have got lost along this path again and again, quite deliberately. I wasn't searching for a strong sensation; I expected the space to tell me one of its many stories. It's the account of strong presences which live through the destinies of the places. Presences that are able to touch you with their silent energy.

*Venezia/Marghera* (Venice Biennial), Milan: Charta, 1997

Naples, 1990. Castel Sant'Elmo.

Herculaneum, 1985. Athletes from the Villa of the Papyri.

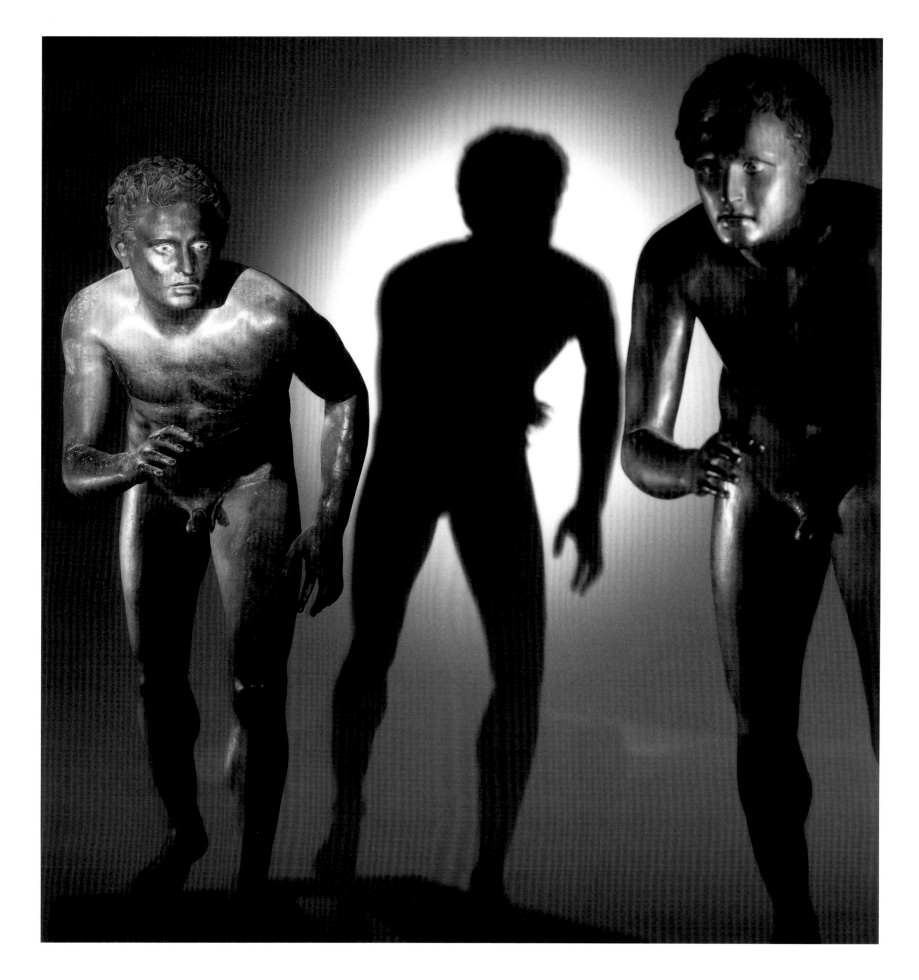

Naples, 1979. Virgil's school.

San Marino, 1989.

Syracuse, 1987. Latomie (Greek quarries).

Naples, 2005. Main archives building.

Rome, 2005. Villa Gordiani.

Paestum, 1985.

Adda, 1999. River structures.

Bolzano, 1995. Dominican cloister.

Turin, 2005. Corso Cairoli.

Venice, 1986. Molino Stucky.

Chieti, 1995. Chemical factory.

Erbusco, 2003.

Bolzano, 1995. Strada del Renon.

*Overleaf*
*Left:* Padula, 1985. Certosa di San Lorenzo.
*Right:* Bolzano, 1995. Chiesa dei Francescani.

Pozzuoli, 1990. Flavian amphitheatre.

Gaggiano, 1992. San Invenzio Church.

Brescia, 1987. Rocca d'Anfo fortress.

Sperlonga, 1993.

Sila, 1999. Lake Ampollino.

Stromboli, 1999.

These images are fragments which help to enrich the mosaic of the story – visions that complete a long exploration of memory which is at the root of my work. Accounts of things that have already passed or have yet to take place; a way of driving out the doubts and uneasiness of living.

*Milano senza confini*, Milan: Silvana editoriale, 2000

Naples, 1997. Real Albergo dei Poveri.

Pozzuoli, 1993. Flavian amphitheatre.

Pozzuoli, 1993. Roman necropolis

Milan, 1999. Castello Sforzesco.

Naples, 2005. Pio Monte della Misericordia.

Vigevano, 1999. Stables at Castello Sforzesco.

Bolzano, 1995. Gasteiner gym.

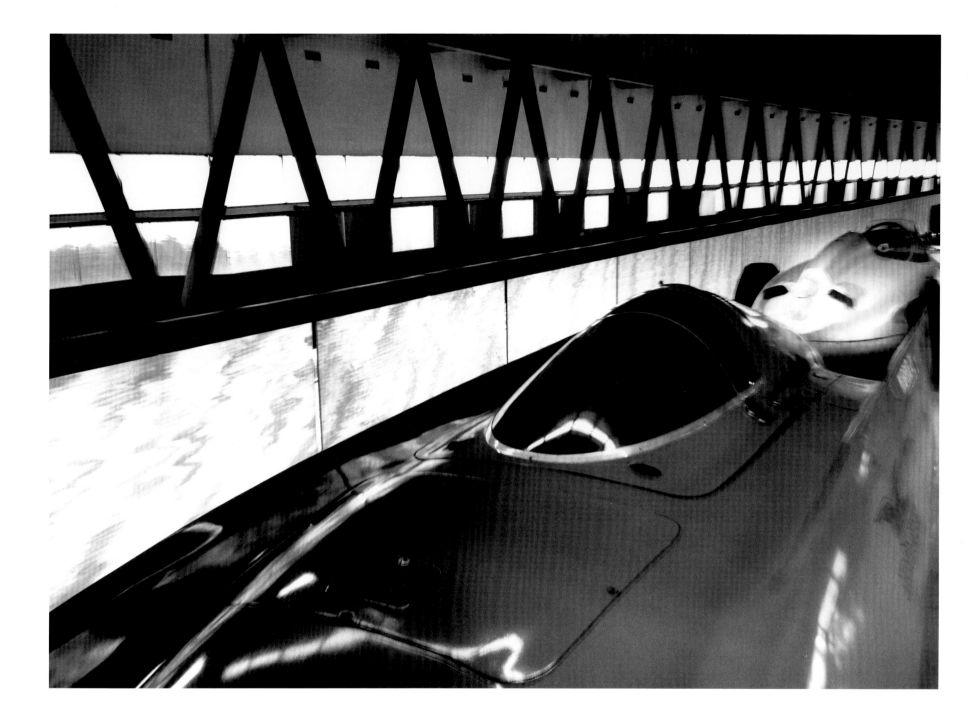

Turin, 1998. Motor Museum.

Naples, 1997. Real Albergo dei Poveri.

Pompeii, 1982.

Rome, 2005. EUR suburb.

Milan, 1999. Colonne di San Lorenzo.

Turin, 2005. Fiat Mirafiori plant.

Rome, 2006. Tiber Island.

Milan, 1999. Castello Sforzesco.

Turin, 2005. Academy of Sciences.

Pompeii, 1982. Casa degli Amorini Dorati.

Turin, 2005. Museum of Human Anatomy.

Naples, 1995. Santa Chiara Museum.

Naples, 1981. Certosa di San Martino.

Carpi, 1990. Museo Monumento al Deportato.

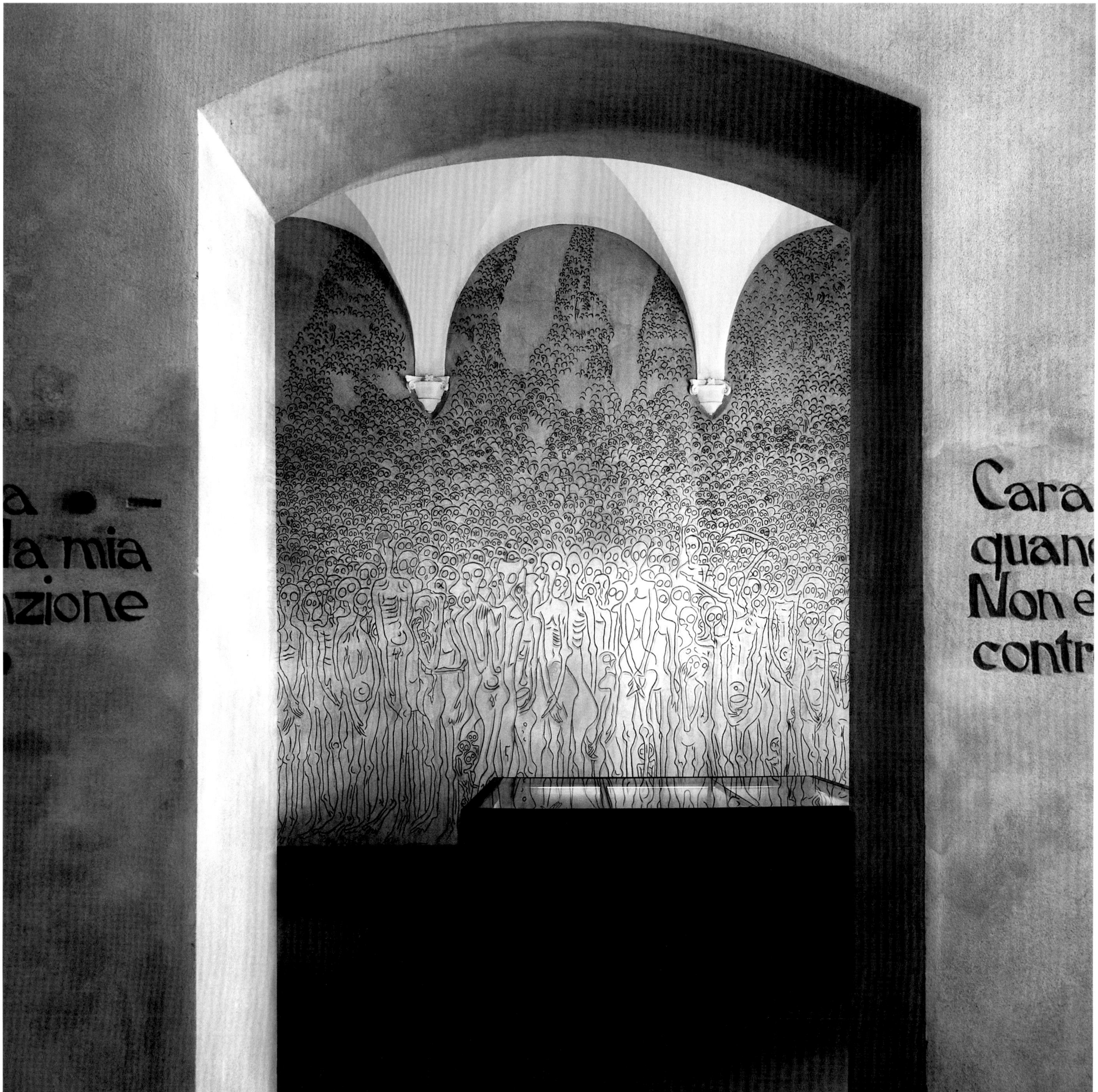
a
la mia
azione
Cara
Non

Genoa, 2002. Flyover.

Lecce, 1986.

Turin, 2005. State Archives.

Rimini, 1987.

Turin, 2005. Piazza Vittorio Veneto.

Milan, 1999. Cathedral.

Torre del Greco, 1980.

Every one of my works is born from a moment of emotion. Each of my photos is the result of an occasional encounter that imparts to me a particular state of mind. It is as if the images, that have almost never been related to people but to landscapes, forms, materials and light, were prepared for me and they were always there waiting for me.

*European Eyes on Japan*, Tokyo: Ed. EU-Japan Fest, 2003

Naples, 1997. Real Albergo dei Poveri.

Matera, 1988. Cathedral carved into the rock.

Naples, 1981. San Paolo Maggiore.

Naples, 1986. Suor Orsola.

Naples, 1986. Suor Orsola.

Milan, 2000. Chiaravalle Abbey.

Capri, 1984. Villa Sarah.

Salemi (Trapani), 1983.
Maltese cottage.

Rome, 2006. Villa Medici.

Trieste, 1985. Risiera di San Sabba, site of a prison and death camp during the Second World War.

Milan, 2001. Bicocca campus.

Otranto, 1988. Cathedral.

Bolzano, 1995. Casa del Torchio.

Pescara, 2002.

Naples, 1987. Centro Antico.

Naples, 1982. Coroglio.

Paestum, 1985.

Sabbioneta, 1999. Ancient Theatre.

Salemi (Trapani), 1983. Villa Scurto.

Gibellina, 1982.

*Overleaf*
*Left:* Turin, 2005. Palatine Gate.
*Right:* Gibellina, 1981.

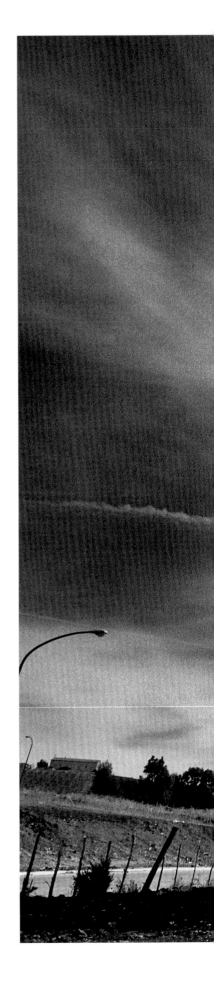

Adriatic Riviera, 2000.

Stromboli, 1999.

Stromboli, 1999.

Naples, 2000.

My photographs reflect my thoughts and testify to the discomfort and disquiet I feel towards our time. Perceptions of bewilderment and disorientation also aim to express an idea of escape from reality.

*Città Visibili/Visible Cities*, conversation with Hans Ulrich Obrist, Milan: Charta, 2006

Salemi (Trapani), 1983. Chiesa Madre.

Naples, 1980. Centro Antico.

Messina, 1992. Alcantara Gorges.

Acitrezza, 1992. Stacks.

San Marino, 1990.

Naples, 1988. Santa Chiara Monastery.

Bitonto, 1997.

Rome, 2006. Circus of Maxentius.

Ravenna, 1989.

Pompeii, 1982. Western insula.

Naples, 1996. Sottosuolo, an ancient network of underground caverns and passageways beneath the city.

*Preceding pages*
*Left:* Rome, 2006. Palazzo Farnese.

*Right:* Bergamo, 1997.

Bolzano, 1995. Via Sassari.

Naples, 1982. Piazza Mercato.

Turin, 2005. Accademia Albertina.

Genoa, 2000. Flyover.

Matera, 1984.

Civita di Bagnoregio, 1988.

Gaggiano, 1992. Large farmstead.

Acitrezza, 1992. Stacks.

Lipari, 1999.

Naples, 1990. View.

I embarked on this journey with the belief that I would be exploring a real place…but as it turned out, the camera's purpose, which should have been to 'look out', to reflect reality, was ultimately to 'look within' and project into the world a timeless dimension.

*Isolario mediterraneo*, Milan: Federico Motta, 2000

Cumae, 1985. Cave of the Cumaean Sibyl.

*Overleaf*
*Left:* Pozzuoli, 1993. Flavian amphitheatre.
*Right:* Baia, 1993. Companion of Ulysses.

Pozzuoli, 1985. Solfatara.

Rome, 2006. View from the Palatine.

Herculaneum, 1999.

Rome, 2005. Forum of Augustus.

Cremona, 2000. Soncino Castle.

Salemi (Trapani), 1983. Baglio Ranchibile.

San Marino, 1989.

Naples, 1997. Real Albergo dei Poveri.

Porto Marghera (Venice), 1996. Industrial zone.

Campi Flegrei, 1990. Lake Fusaro.

Naples, 1980.

Olbia, 2000. Punta Pedrosa.

Baia, 1993. Apollo.

Porto Marghera (Venice), 1996. Industrial zone.

Agrigento, 1993.

Naples, 1997. Real Albergo dei Poveri.

Pompeii, 1983. Western insula.

Marechiaro (Naples), 1999.

Brindisi, 1994. Enichem plant.

Orio Litta, 1999. Villa Cavazzi.

Stromboli, 1999.

Sybaris, 2000.

# A Biographical Account

## Roberta Valtorta

The second of four children, Mimmo Jodice was born in the La Sanità district of Naples on 29 March 1934. His father died when he was a child. Although the young Jodice went straight into work after primary school, he continued to study privately and was passionately interested in the arts, theatre, classical music and jazz, assiduously teaching himself to paint and draw. At the end of the 1950s he started to take photographs.

In 1962 Jodice married Angela Salomone, lifelong companion, esteemed collaborator, and mother of his three children, Barbara (b. 1963), Francesco (b. 1963) and Sebastiano (b. 1971). He bought his first magnifier in 1964. It was during this period that he went to the Academy of Fine Arts in Naples, where an avant-garde revival was under way, and he began to experiment with different materials, abstract forms, and with the linguistic and technical aspects of photography, perceiving its role as a form of expression rather than a vehicle for mere narrative. Nudes and portraits were his preferred subjects, but he was also drawn to everyday objects, which he reinterpreted within abstract compositions, sometimes with a hint of Cubism.

In 1967 he decided to concentrate on photography. His works were exhibited for the first time at the Libreria La Mandragola in Naples, and he had his first photograph published, in the Italian issue of *Popular Photography* magazine. At Domenico Rea's house he met Allen Ginsberg and Fernanda Pivano. The prevailing climate of cultural, political and social change during that era prompted Jodice to use photography as an art form and explore new depths, whilst continuing to experiment with different techniques and materials.

urbino
teatro spento
12-20 novembre 68
fotografie di mimmo jodice

Invitation to an exhibition at Teatro Spento, Urbino, 1968.

Jodice mounted an exhibition at the Teatro Spento in Urbino in 1968. It was the year that also marked his entry into the art world, with the formation of a long and successful collaboration with the Neapolitan gallerist Lucio Amelio, along with others such as Lia Rumma. They introduced him to some of the most important exponents of the avant-garde, including Andy Warhol, Robert Rauschenberg, Joseph Beuys, Gino De Dominicis, Giulio Paolini, Josef Kosuth, Vito Acconci, Mario Merz, Jannis Kounellis, Sol LeWitt and Hermann Nitsch. His close contact with this world opened his eyes to the sense of urgency that marked those years of renewal and protest. This realization manifested itself in new photographic experiments, and the documentation of many of the artistic events taking place, which were later published in the book *Mimmo Jodice: Avanguardie a Napoli dalla contestazione al riflusso* (1996). Through Lucio Amelio, he also got to know Filiberto Menna, Achille Bonito Oliva, Angelo Trimarco and Germano Celant, who all later wrote about his work.

Mimmo Jodice with Jannis Kounellis, Naples, 1969. Photograph by Lucio Amelio.

Mimmo Jodice with a group of young people at Sicof, Milan, 1982. Photograph by Giorgio Lotti.

Mimmo Jodice with Andy Warhol and Joseph Beuys, Naples, 1976. Photograph by Antonio Troncone.

Jodice became friends with musicologist Roberto De Simone, an expert in popular traditions, in 1969. Their friendship sparked in Jodice an interest in the festivals and religious ceremonies of Naples and the south of Italy, and a passion for anthropological study. In 1974 they co-published the book *Chi è devoto: Feste popolari in Campania*. In 1970 Jodice was invited to run experimental courses at the Academy of Fine Arts in Naples (he was professor of photography there between 1975 and 1994) and became the leading authority on Neapolitan photography, then still in its infancy, and southern Italian photography as a whole. He exhibited at Lanfranco Colombo's Galleria Il Diaframma in Milan as part of Cesare Zavattini's show, 'Nudo dentro cartelle ermetiche'. During those years, his work was a cross between artistic construction and social realism.

Mimmo Jodice with Andy Warhol, Naples, 1976.

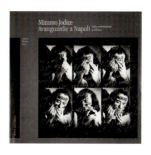

*Avanguardie a Napoli dalla contestazione al riflusso*, Milan: Federico Motta, 1996.

*Nudi dentro cartelle ermetiche*, Milan: Il Diaframma, 1970.

Jodice met Cesare De Seta in 1971, with whom he shared a studio in Naples until 1988. The outbreak of cholera in the city that same year made him focus on social conditions, compelling him to go beyond simply chronicling these events, to confront the underlying misery and degradation. The results were exhibited in 'Il ventre del colera', mounted at Sicof in Milan in 1973; the sociologist Domenico De Masi contributed text.

In 1974 Jodice travelled to Japan. He also held a show at Galleria Il Diaframma, in which he juxtaposed his photographs with postcards. The book *Mezzogiorno: Questione aperta*, an extensive work exploring social conditions in the south of Italy, was published the following year. Jodice's social photography started to move away from traditional reportage in search of social types, symbolic figures and scenarios, set against a backdrop of particular locations and urban spaces.

*Chi è devoto: Feste popolari in Campania*, Naples: Edizioni Scientifiche Italiane, 1974.

Meanwhile Jodice continued to strive for a greater purity of language in his photography. For 'Identificazione', an important show mounted by Marina Miraglia at Studio Trisorio, Naples, in 1978, Jodice collected a series of images taken by photographers whom he particularly admired, including Avedon, Kertész, Evans and Brandt. In addition, the magazine *Progresso Fotografico* dedicated a monograph to him, *La Napoli di Mimmo Jodice*, with texts by Giuseppe Alario, Percy Allum, Domenico De Masi, Cesare De Seta and Pier Paolo Preti. The following year Jodice contributed his series *Strappi e momenti sovrapposti* to the exhibition 'Iconicittà/1: Una visione sul reale' at Palazzo Massari, Ferrara.

Jodice's period of social photography drew to a close in 1980 with the book *Mimmo Jodice: Vedute di Napoli*, which included an essay by Giuseppe Bonini. He started to develop a new perspective in which the human figure was no longer the protagonist, concentrating instead on empty, menacing, urban spaces, laden with memories and metaphysical presences. In the early 1980s, the collaboration between Jodice and Cesare De Seta led to the launch of an ambitious cultural project, promoted by the Azienda Autonoma di Soggiorno di Napoli, whose function was to explore the multifaceted nature of life in contemporary Naples. Many different photographers from Italy and further afield contributed to the project, including Mario Cresci, Luigi Ghirri, Lee Friedlander, Claude Nori, Guido Guidi, Gabriele Basilico, Paul den Hollander, Arnaud Claass, Manfred Willmann, Joan Fontcuberta and Vincenzo Castella. The first exhibition in the series, and the book that accompanied it, bore the title 'Napoli 1981: Sette fotografi per una nuova immagine'.

*Vedute di Napoli*, Milan: Mazzotta, 1980.

During this period he also established closer ties with the world of architecture, working with the likes of Vittorio Magnago Lampugnani, Italo Lupi, Pier Luigi Nicolin, Nicola Di Battista and Álvaro Siza, as well as George Vallet, who introduced him to archaeology – a discipline that would profoundly influence his work. In 1981 Jodice contributed to the exhibition 'Facets of the Permanent Collection: Expressions of the Human Condition', curated by Van Deren Coke for the San Francisco Museum of Modern Art, along with William Klein, Diane Arbus, Larry Clark and Lisette Model.

Mimmo Jodice with Bernard Plossu, Paris, 1994.

Three further titles were published in 1982: *Teatralità quotidiana a Napoli*, *Naples: une archéologie future*, with an introduction by Jean Claude Lemagny, and *Gibellina*, in which Jodice examines the traces that man has left on the landscape in the past, and interprets them as a sign of what is to come. It was during this same period that he got to know Jean Digne, director of the French Institute in Naples, and his friendship with the French photographer Bernard Plossu grew deeper. In 1983, the Gruppo

*Naples: une archéologie future*, Paris: Institut Culturel Italien, 1982.

Editoriale Fabbri brought out a book on Jodice's work as part of its series on great photographers, for which Filiberto Menna wrote some of the text.

In 1983 Cesare De Seta supervised the *Capri* project, which was commissioned by the Italian television network RAI from Jodice and a friend of his, Luigi Ghirri, a fellow photographer whom he had known for three years. The project involved extensive research into new ways of understanding the contemporary landscape in Italy, an idea that was consolidated the following year with the collective exhibition (and catalogue of the same name) 'Viaggio in Italia', and then again in 1986 with 'Esplorazioni sulla via Emilia'. Both were the brainchild of Luigi Ghirri.

*Mimmo Jodice*, 'I Grandi Fotografi' series, Milan: Gruppo Editoriale Fabbri, 1983.

Between 1984 and 1986 Jodice collaborated with Ghirri, Gabriele Basilico, Giovanni Chiaramonte, Guido Guidi, Olivo Barbieri, Mario Cresci, Vincenzo Castella, Vittore Fossati and others who had been involved in 'Viaggio in Italia', as well as the likes of Arnaud Claass, Bernard Descamps, Georges Rousse and John Hilliard, on many different collective exhibitions and public commissions, both in Italy (Trieste, Carpi, Rome) and further afield (Orléans, Barcelona, Paris, Toronto).

In 1984 Jodice took part in the exhibition 'Images et imaginaire d'architecture' at the Centre Pompidou in Paris. In 1985 he was involved in a project on the ancient city of Paestum, which subsequently became the focus of an exhibition (1986) at the Federal Hall National Memorial, New York, to which Angelo Trimarco contributed. An important exhibition on Jodice's hometown also took place in 1985, accompanied by a book of the same name: *Un secolo di furore: L'espressività del Seicento a Napoli*, with an introduction by Nicola Spinosa, head of the Soprintendenza per i Beni Artistici e Storici department in Naples. In the exhibition Jodice reinterpreted fragments of the Baroque paintings by Caravaggio, Ribera, Caracciolo and Giordano with emotive poignancy.

He began *Archivio dello Spazio* in 1987, a huge project commissioned by the Province of Milan which marked the start of a ten-year-long collaboration. It was devised to study the relationship between architecture and the industrialized landscape around the city, the capital of the Lombardy region of Italy. In the same year, Jodice participated with Paolo Gioli, Christian Milovanoff, John Stathatos, Alain Fleischer and Javier Vallhonrat in the collective exhibition 'Mémoires de l'origine', which was curated by Jean-François Chevrier and held at the Centre de la Vieille Charité, Marseilles. Three important books were published around this time: *Suor Orsola: Cittadella monastica nella Napoli del Seicento* (1987), *Napoli sospesa* (1988), with a text by Arturo Carlo Quintavalle,

*Suor Orsola: Cittadella monastica nella Napoli del Seicento*, Milan: Mazzotta, 1987.

Mimmo and Angela Jodice with Álvaro Siza, Porto, Portugal, 1990.

and *Mimmo Jodice: Fotografie* (1988), with an introduction by Carlo Bertelli. The latter was accompanied by an exhibition as part of the 'Mois de la Photo' event in Paris. Another book by Jodice, published in 1988, contained photographs of the city of Arles.

During these years a double thread ran through Jodice's work: on the one hand, a surreal and ethereal vision of

Naples, and on the other, an obsession with the imprints of the past on the present, and with the roots of Mediterranean culture. His study of architecture and the ancient world was reinforced by his work as a photographer of art, working alongside important archaeologists and art historians such as Eugenio Battisti, Giulio Carlo Argan, Giuliano Briganti and Fausto Zevi. A number of important publications were born of these close collaborations, including *Michelangelo scultore* (1989), *Paestum* (1990), *Pompei* (1991–92), *Antonio Canova* (1992) and *Neapolis* (1994). In these works, Jodice

*La città invisibile*, Naples: Electa, 1990.

The exhibition 'Tempo interiore' at Palazzo della Ragione, Padua, 1994.

Opening of the exhibition 'Mediterranean' at the Philadelphia Museum of Art, 1995. From left to right, Michael Hoffman, director of Aperture, Francesco Jodice, Mimmo and Angela Jodice.

captures the solemnity of the museum pieces, at the same time imbuing them with a timeless quality.

In 1990 an exhibition at the Fundação de Serralves in Porto, Portugal, featured Jodice's photographs of Álvaro Siza's modernist masterpieces. A close working relationship had been developing between Jodice and the Portuguese architect for a number of years. Jodice also published another book on Naples, *La città invisibile: Nuove vedute di Napoli*, compiled by Germano Celant. He collaborated with Tom Drahos, Christian Milovanoff, Jean-Louis Garnell and others on the collective exhibition 'Vue du pont' at Chartreuse de Villeneuve-lez-Avignon, which reinforced Jodice's interest in the themes of memory and the ancient world – themes that reoccurred in 1992 in his work for the project *Musa museu*, commissioned by the Ayuntamiento de Barcelona. Other artists with whom he collaborated on the project included Gabriele Basilico, Manel Esclusa, Paul den Hollander, Humberto Rivas, Tony Catany, Pere Formiguera, Joan Fontcuberta and Javier Vallhonrat. In 1993 his monograph *Tempo interiore*, edited by Roberta Valtorta, was published in French and Italian and accompanied by a large-scale exhibition at Villa Pignatelli, Naples, and subsequently Palazzo della Ragione, Padua. He also participated in a number of other important collective exhibitions in Italy ('Muri di carta'

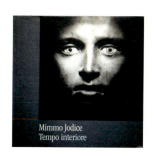

*Tempo interiore*, Milan: Federico Motta, 1993.

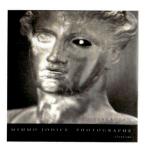

*Mediterranean*, New York: Aperture, 1995.

at the Venice Biennial, curated by Arturo Carlo Quintavalle; and 'Immagini italiane' at the Guggenheim in Venice, curated by Melissa Harris) and elsewhere ('Jardins do Paraíso' in Coimbra, Portugal, curated by Gabriel Bauret; and *Genius Loci* in Joinville, France, curated by Chantal Grande).

In 1994, together with Gabriele Basilico and Olivo Barbieri, Jodice was commissioned to create a photographic view of Modena, which resulted in the catalogue *Gli occhi sulla*

*Paris: City of Light*, New York: Maison Européenne de la Photographie/Aperture, 1998.

The exhibition 'Eden' at Palazzo Ducale, Mantua, 1998.

*città* and exhibition; and in New York some of his experimental works from the 1960s went on display at the Solomon Guggenheim Museum as part of the collective exhibition 'The Italian Metamorphosis 1943–1968', curated by Germano Celant.

A year later, Jodice became firmly established on the international scene when *Mediterranean* was published in the US, Italy and Germany, with texts by George Hersey and Predrag Matvejevic; this was followed by an important exhibition which toured the Philadelphia Museum of Art, the Cleveland Museum of Art, the Triennial in Milan, the Pinacoteca Provinciale in Bari, Castello di Rivoli, Aperture's Burden Gallery in New York, and Arles. The book marked another turning point

*Eden*, Milan: Leonardo Arte, 1998.

*Isolario mediterraneo*, Milan: Federico Motta, 2000.

in terms of Jodice's style, which was moving away from documentary and becoming increasingly pictorial. In 1997 he took part in a project by Paolo Costantini, entitled *Venezia / Marghera: Fotografia e trasformazione della città contemporanea.*

In 1998 *Paris: City of Light* was published, which focused on the historic and monumental aspects of the French capital, as well as its role as a modern metropolis. It was accompanied by an exhibition at the Maison Européenne de la Photographie

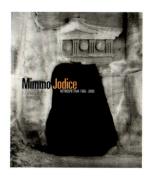

Mimmo Jodice: Retrospettiva 1965–2000, Turin: Edizioni GAM, 2001.

in Paris. *Eden* came out the same year, with an introduction by Germano Celant; this work was also the subject of an exhibition at the Museo di Palazzo Ducale in Mantua, which revealed Jodice's renewed interest in everyday objects, displayed in blurred and surreal settings.

In 1999 *Reale Albergo dei Poveri* was published. This book was dedicated to the extraordinary eighteenth-century Real Albergo dei Poveri – formerly a hospice/almshouse – in Naples and was accompanied by an exhibition at the Cappella Palatina di Castelnuovo near Naples. He also contributed to Roberta Valtorta's *Milano senza confini*, which was accompanied by a collective exhibition with Gabriele Basilico, Paolo Gioli, Guido Guidi, Vincenzo Castella, Thomas Struth, Peter Fischli, David Weiss, John Davies, Paul Graham and Manfred Willmann at Spazio Oberdan in Milan.

'Anamnesi' at the National Gallery of Modern Art, Rome, 2000.

A further two books came out in 2000: *Isolario mediterraneo*, which focused on the solitude and absoluteness of seascapes, with text by Predrag Matvejevic, and *Old Calabria: I luoghi del Grand Tour*. The exhibition 'Fate presto!' also took place, with a book of the same name. Twenty years after the devastating Campania–Basilicata earthquake, this project brought together a collection of photographs by some of the most renowned figures in the field, including Mario Cresci, Luciano D'Alessandro, Mario De Biasi, Vito Falcone, Mauro Galligani, Gianni Giansanti, Roberto Koch, Giorgio Lotti and Jodice himself. Jodice's own exhibition, 'Anamnesi', was shown at the National Gallery of Modern Art in Rome, and he participated in the exhibition

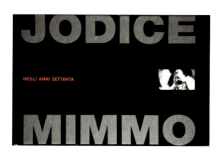

Negli anni Settanta, Milan: Baldini & Castoldi, 2001.

*Inlands: Visions of Boston*, Milan: Skira, 2001.

'Luoghi come paesaggi' at the Uffizi in Florence, which highlighted the effects of public commissions on the European landscape during the 1980s and 1990s.

In 2001, the exhibition 'Mimmo Jodice: Retrospettiva 1965–2000' was mounted at the Galleria Civica d'Arte Moderna e Contemporanea di Torino (GAM), Turin; Pier Giovanni Castagnoli compiled the catalogue, which included texts by Roberta Valtorta and Paul Virilio. The book *Gli iconemi: storia e memoria del paesaggio* – a visual journey through the plains of Lombardy, commissioned by the Region of Lombardy – was also published, followed by an exhibition (2002) at Palazzo Bagatti Valsecchi in Milan. Jodice was also invited by the Massachusetts Institute of Technology in Boston, in collaboration with Harvard University, to undertake a project on Milan. In April of that year, the Italian architect Gae Aulenti enlarged some of Jodice's archaeological photographs for the underground station Museo in Naples. In October, as part of 'Modena per la Fotografia', he exhibited some 'socially aware' photographs from the 1970s. Coinciding with the festival came the publication of a monograph entitled *Mimmo Jodice: Negli anni Settanta*, edited by Filippo Maggia. The following month Jodice exhibited a series of photographs of the sea in the Milanese branch of Galleria Lia Rumma.

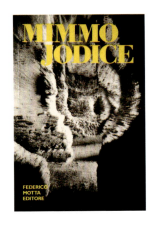

*Mimmo Jodice*, Milan: Federico Motta, 2003.

He also took part in the exhibition 'An Eye for the City' at the University of New Mexico Art Museum, curated by Antonella Russo. Jodice's work on Boston was exhibited at the Massachusetts College of Art in 2001; entitled 'Inlands: Visions of Boston', the exhibition was accompanied by a book of the same name.

In 2002 he was invited to take part in the exhibition celebrating the fiftieth anniversary of

*São Paulo*, Milan: Skira, 2004.

*Mimmo Jodice dalla collezione Cotroneo*, Milan: Skira, 2004.

the Aperture Foundation in New York, along with another exhibition marking the fifteenth anniversary of Condé Nast, also in New York. He was also part of the exhibition 'La natura morta: Da Manet ai giorni nostri' at the Gallery of Modern Art in Bologna, and exhibited his work on the sea at the Musée de la Mer in Cannes, under the title 'Silence'. In that same year, Jodice was acknowledged for his work in the fields of art history, literature and culture in general: his photographs were included in a new edition of *Arte Moderna* by Giulio Carlo Argan, revised by the respected art critic Achille Bonito Oliva, as well as in an Einaudi edition of *The Tragedies of Euripides* which incorporated a series of photographs from *Mediterranean* as a visual counterpart to the words of the Greek tragedian.

Jodice was entered into the *Enciclopedia Universale dell'Arte Garzanti* and the *Enciclopedia Treccani* in 2003. In addition, his work on the sea was exhibited at the Galerie Baudoin Lebon in Paris, and the anthology *Mimmo Jodice* was published, edited by Roberta Valtorta. The Accademia Nazionale dei Lincei acknowledged Jodice's work in the photographic field by awarding him the Antonio Feltrinelli prize – the first time it had been awarded to a photographer.

In 2004 he was amongst the contributors to the book *Michael E. Hoffman: Outside the Ordinary. A Tribute in Pictures*, which was published in remembrance of Michael E. Hoffman, long-time director at the Aperture Foundation publishing house. Many key photographers from around the world donated their images, which are now in the collection of the Philadelphia Museum of Art. The Museu de Arte de São Paulo dedicated an important exhibition to Jodice, consisting of photographs of the city which had been commissioned to mark the 450th anniversary of São Paulo's foundation.

*Città Visibili/Visible Cities*, Milan: Charta, 2006.

His work was also exhibited at the Museum of Modern and Contemporary Art in Rovereto, and now forms part of the Cotroneo collection at the museum. Exhibitions were also mounted at the Museum of Modern Art in Wakayama, Japan, and at the Moscow House of Photography, during its biennial of photography.

With the construction of the underground railway in Turin in 2005, the city's Gallery of Modern Art invited Jodice to participate in the project *Sei per Torino*, along with Olivo Barbieri, Gabriele Basilico, Franco Fontana, Armin Linke and Jodice's son Francesco, an artist in his own right. He also contributed to a project on the city of Naples, commissioned by the Soprintendenza per i Beni Architettonici e il Paesaggio and by the Patrimonio Storico Artistico ed Etnoantropologico in the city. This collaboration led to the publication of the book *Obiettivo Napoli: Luoghi memorie immagini*, with photographs by Mimmo Jodice, Gabriele Basilico, Luca Campigotto, Vincenzo Castella, Pino Musi and Eiko Hosoe.

In 2006 Jodice was involved in a collective exhibition on Italian art and design at the Musée des Beaux-Arts in Montreal, entitled 'Il modo italiano: Design et avant-garde en Italie au XX$^{\text{ème}}$ siècle', and then in 2007 at MART in Rovereto. Other exhibitions during this period included 'Light' (2005) at the Gallery of Modern Art in Bologna, curated by Valerio Dehò, and 'Mito mediterraneo' (2006) at the Italian Institute of Culture in Tokyo; 'Mediterranean' – undoubtedly one of Jodice's most important and best-loved projects – was mounted at the Moscow House of Photography, and he also took part in the collective exhibition 'Italy Made in Art: Now' at the Museum of Contemporary Art in Shanghai (both 2006). Towards the end of 2006, the Università degli Studi Federico II in Naples awarded him an honorary degree in architecture, in recognition of the many years he has devoted to this subject, and his creative interpretations of architecture and the complexity of urban and metropolitan spaces through the medium of photography. To mark the

Mimmo Jodice is awarded an honorary degree in architecture at the Università degli Studi di Napoli Federico II, 2006.

With his family at the degree ceremony. From left to right: his son Francesco, daughter Barbara, Mimmo, wife Angela and son Sebastiano.

occasion, the Palazzo Reale in Naples mounted an exhibition of his photographs of major cities such as New York, Tokyo, São Paulo, Rome, Boston, Paris, Moscow and Naples. The exhibition was accompanied by a book, *Città Visibili/Visible Cities,* with text contributions by Benedetto Gravagnuolo, head of the Faculty of Architecture, Hans Ulrich Obrist and Stefano Boeri. This is another theme that has been much favoured by Jodice, particularly in recent years.

During 2007 he was involved in a series of commissions for *Sguardi gardesani,* which led to an exhibition and catalogue (edited by Walter Guadagnini). Jodice's research into locations around Lake Garda was conducted with his friend of many years and fellow photographer Bernard Plossu.

# Monographs

Mimmo Jodice, *Nudi dentro cartelle ermetiche*, introduction by Cesare Zavattini, catalogue to the exhibition at Galleria il Diaframma, Milan, 1970

*Chi è devoto: Feste popolari in Campania*, text by Roberto De Simone, photographs by Mimmo Jodice, preface by Carlo Levi, Naples: Edizioni Scientifiche Italiane, 1974

*La Napoli di Mimmo Jodice*, monograph issue of *Progresso Fotografico*, no. 1, Milan, January 1978, texts by Giuseppe Alario, Percy Allum, Domenico De Masi, Cesare De Seta, Pier Paolo Preti, Mimmo Jodice

Alberto Piovani (ed.), *Mimmo Jodice: Vedute di Napoli*, text by Giuseppe Bonini, introduction by Giuseppe Galasso, Milan: Mazzotta, 1980

Mimmo Jodice, *Gibellina*, texts by Pier Luigi Nicolin and Arturo Carlo Quintavalle, Milan: Electa, 1982

*Joseph Beuys: Natale a Gibellina*, photographs by Mimmo Jodice, text by Claudio Abbate, Comune di Gibellina, 1982

Mimmo Jodice, *Teatralità quotidiana a Napoli*, text by Saverio Vertone, Naples: Guida, 1982

Mimmo Jodice, *Naples: une archéologie future*, introduction by Jean Claude Lemagny, text by Giuseppe Bonini, Paris: Institut Culturel Italien, 1982

*Mimmo Jodice*, texts by Giuseppe Alario and Filiberto Menna, 'I Grandi Fotografi' series, Milan: Gruppo Editoriale Fabbri, 1983

Mimmo Jodice, *Qui come altrove: San Martino Valle Caudina*, introduction by Gianni Raviele, Rome: Edizioni della Cometa, 1985

Mimmo Jodice, *Un secolo di furore: L'espressività del Seicento a Napoli*, text by Nicola Spinosa, Rome: Edizioni Editer, 1985

Mimmo Jodice, *Suor Orsola: Cittadella monastica nella Napoli del Seicento*, texts by Antonio Vilani, Elena Croce, Luigi Firpo, Claudio Magris, Annette Malochet, Milan: Mazzotta, 1987

Mimmo Jodice, *Arles*, preface by Michèle Moutashar, Arles: Musées d'Arles, 1988

Mimmo Jodice, *Napoli sospesa*, texts by Arturo Carlo Quintavalle and Vittorio Magnago Lampugnani, Rome: Synchron, 1988

*Mimmo Jodice: Fotografie*, introduction by Carlo Bertelli, Naples: Electa, 1988

Mimmo Jodice, *I percorsi della memoria*, texts by Georges Vallet and Franco Lefevre, Rome: Synchron, 1990

Mimmo Jodice, *La città invisibile: Nuove vedute di Napoli*, text by Germano Celant, Naples: Electa, 1990

Mimmo Jodice, *Paesaggi*, text by Gabriele Perretta, Rome: La Nuova Pesa, 1992

Mimmo Jodice, *Confini*, Rome: Incontri Internazionali d'Arte, 1992

Roberta Valtorta (ed.), *Mimmo Jodice: Tempo interiore*, Milan: Federico Motta Editore, 1993; French edition *Passé intérieur*, Paris: Contrejour, 1993

Mimmo Jodice, *Mediterranean*, texts by George Hersey and Predrag Matvejevic, New York: Aperture, 1995; Italian edition, Udine: Art&, 1995; German edition, Munich: Knesebeck, 1995

Mimmo Jodice, *Avanguardie a Napoli dalla contestazione al riflusso*, text by Bruno Corà, Milan: Federico Motta Editore, 1996

Mimmo Jodice, *Paris: City of Light*, text by Adam Gopnik, New York: Maison Européenne de la Photographie/Aperture, 1998

Mimmo Jodice, *Eden*, text by Germano Celant, Milan: Leonardo Arte, 1998

Mimmo Jodice, *Reale Albergo dei Poveri*, introduction by Antonio Bassolino, Milan: Federico Motta Editore, 1999

Mimmo Jodice/Predrag Matvejevic, *Isolario Mediterraneo*, Milan: Federico Motta Editore, 2000

Mimmo Jodice, *Old Calabria: I luoghi del Grand Tour*, text by Giuseppe Merlino, Milan: Federico Motta Editore, 2000

Pier Giovanni Castagnoli (ed.), *Mimmo Jodice: Retrospettiva 1965–2000*, texts by Pier Giovanni Castagnoli, Paul Virilio, Roberta Valtorta, Turin: Galleria Civica d'Arte Moderna e Contemporanea, 2001

Filippo Maggia (ed.), *Mimmo Jodice: Negli anni Settanta*, Milan: Baldini & Castoldi, 2001

David D. Nolta and Ellen R. Shapiro (eds), *Inlands: Visions of Boston*, Milan: Skira, 2001

*Mimmo Jodice: Silence*, texts by Maria Wallet and Erri De Luca, Cannes: Musée de la Mer, 2002

*Mimmo Jodice: Mer*, text by Bernard Millet, Paris: Baudoin Lebon, 2003

Roberta Valtorta (ed.), *Mimmo Jodice*, Milan: Federico Motta Editore, 2003

Giorgio Verzotti (ed.), *Mimmo Jodice dalla collezione Cotroneo*, Milan: Skira, 2004

Mimmo Jodice, *São Paulo*, text by Stefano Boeri, Milan: Skira, 2004

Mimmo Jodice, *Light*, texts by Walter Guadagnini and Valerio Dehò, Bologna: Damiani Editore, 2005

Mimmo Jodice, *Città visibili/Visible Cities*, texts by Benedetto Gravagnuolo, Mimmo Jodice, Hans Ulrich Obrist, Stefano Boeri, Milan: Charta, 2006

# Collaborative Works

Alessandro Petriccione (ed.), *Mezzogiorno: Questione aperta*, coordination by Cesarc Dc Seta, contributions from Giuseppe Galasso, Augusto Graziani, Mimmo Jodice (photographs), Antonio Palermo, Antonio Napolitano, Domenico De Masi, Cesare De Seta, Tullia Pacini, Bari: Laterza, 1975

*Salemi e il suo territorio*, texts by Francesco Venezia and Gabriele Petrusch, introductory essay by Edoardo Benvenuto, photographs by Mimmo Jodice, Milan: Electa, 1984

Giancarlo Cosenza/Mimmo Jodice, *Procida: Un'architettura del Mediterraneo*, with text by Toti Scialoia, Naples: Clean Edizioni, 1986

*Classicismo di età romana: La collezione Farnese*, texts by Raffaele Aiello, Francis Haskell, Carlo Gasparri, photographs by Mimmo Jodice, Naples: Guida Editori, 1988

*Saverio Dioguardi architetto*, introduction by Marcello Petrignani, Naples: Electa, 1988

*Michelangelo scultore*, texts by Eugenio Battisti, photographs by Mimmo Jodice, Naples: Guida Editori, 1989

AA.VV., *I beni culturali per il futuro di Napoli*, introduction by Francesco Sisinni, photographs by Mimmo Jodice, Naples: Electa, 1990

Fausto Zevi (ed.), *Paestum*, photographs by Mimmo Jodice, Naples: Guida Editori, 1990

*Canova all'Ermitage: Le sculture di San Pietroburgo*, texts by Sergej Androsov, Nina Kosareva, Giuliano Briganti, Elena Bassi, introduction by Giulio Carlo Argan, photographs by Mimmo Jodice, Venice: Marsilio Editori, 1991

Fausto Zevi (ed.), *Pompei*, photographs by Mimmo Jodice, two volumes, Naples: Guida Editori, 1991–92

AA.VV., *Antonio Canova*, photographs by Mimmo Jodice, Venice: Marsilio Editori, 1992

Antonio Giuliano (ed.), *La collezione Boncompagni Ludovisi: Algardi, Bernini e la fortuna dell'antico*, photographs by Mimmo Jodice, Venice: Marsilio Editori, 1992

Fausto Zevi (ed.), *Puteoli*, photographs by Mimmo Jodice, Naples: Guida Editori, 1993

Fausto Zevi (ed.), *Neapolis*, photographs by Mimmo Jodice, Naples: Guida Editori, 1994

Michael McDonough, *Malaparte: A House Like Me*, introduction by Tom Wolfe, photographs by Mimmo Jodice, New York: Verve Editions/Clarkson Potter Publisher, 1999

*Gli iconemi: storia e memoria del paesaggio*, texts by Giorgio Negri, Eugenio Turri, Barbara Capozzi, Walter Guadagnini, Emilio Tadini, photographs by Mimmo Jodice, Milan: Electa, 2001

Anna Beltrametti (ed.), *Euripide: Le tragedie*, translated by Filippo Maria Pontani, with an essay by Diego Lanza, photographs by Mimmo Jodice, Turin: Giulio Einaudi Editore, 2002

# Solo Exhibitions

1967 – Libreria La Mandragola, Naples
1968 – Teatro Spento, Palazzo Ducale, Urbino
1969 – Libreria Deperro, Naples: 'Persona'
1970 – Galleria Il Diaframma, Milan: 'Nudi dentro cartelle ermetiche'
1972 – City Hall, Boston: 'Naples and its Region'
1973 – Sicof, Milan: 'Il ventre del colera'
1974 – Galleria Il Diaframma, Milan: 'Fotografie dal Giappone'
1975 – Galleria Lucio Amelio, Naples
1978 – Studio Trisorio, Naples: 'Identificazione'
1981 – 'Vedute di Napoli': Museo Villa Pignatelli, Naples; then at Galleria Rondanini in Rome
1982 – Biblioteca Marciana, Venice: 'Teatralità quotidiana a Napoli'
1982 – Bibliothèque Nationale, Paris: 'Naples: une archéologie future'
1985 – 'Un secolo di furore': Villa Borghese, Rome; then at Museo Villa Pignatelli in Naples and in 1986 at CERN, Geneva
1986 – Federal Hall National Memorial, New York: 'Paestum'
1988 – 'Mois de la Photo', Galerie FRAC Montparnasse, Paris: 'Spoon River Méditerranée'
1988 – Istituto Suor Orsola, Naples: 'Suor Orsola'
1988 – Musée Reattu, Arles: 'Arles'
1990 – Castel Sant'Elmo, Naples: 'La città invisibile'
1991 – Galleria Forum, Tarragona
1992 – 'Confini': Prague; then at Palazzo Racani Arroni, Spoleto
1992 – Galleria La Nuova Pesa, Rome: 'Paesaggi'
1994 – 'Tempo interiore': Museo Villa Pignatelli, Naples; then in 1995 at Palazzo della Ragione, Padua
1994 – Wan Fung Art Gallery, Beijing
1995 – Galleria Lia Rumma, Naples: 'Eden'
1995 – 'Mediterranean': Philadelphia Museum of Art, Philadelphia; then in 1996 at the Palazzo della Triennale, Milan; in 1997 at the Pinacoteca Provinciale, Bari; in 1999 at Cleveland Museum of Art, Cleveland, and Aperture Burden's Gallery, New York; in 2000 at Castello di Rivoli in Turin
1996 – Museo di Capodimonte, Naples: 'Arti visibili'

1996 – Galerie du Chateau d'Eau, Toulouse
1997 – Galerie Meert-Rihoux, Brussels
1997 – Abbaye de Montmajour, Arles: 'Entre mémoire et histoire'
1998 – Kunstmuseum, Düsseldorf: 'La città invisibile'
1998 – Maison Européenne de la Photographie, Paris: 'Paris: City of Light'
1998 – Museo di Palazzo Ducale, Mantua: 'Eden'
2000 – Galleria Nazionale d'Arte Moderna, Rome: 'Anamnesi'
2000 – Cappella Palatina di Castelnuovo, Naples: 'Il Real Albergo dei Poveri'
2001 – Galleria d'Arte Moderna, Turin: 'Retrospettiva 1965–2000'
2001 – Conde Duque, Madrid: 'Rughe di pietra'
2001 – Massachusetts College of Art, Boston: 'Inlands: Visions of Boston'
2001 – Galleria Lia Rumma, Milan: 'Mare'
2002 – Palazzo Bagatti Valsecchi, Milan: 'Gli iconemi: Storia e memoria del paesaggio'
2002 – Musée de la Mer, Cannes: 'Silence'
2003 – Galerie Baudoin Lebon, Paris: 'Mer'
2004 – Moscow House of Photography, Moscow: 'Paris'
2004 – Museum of Modern Art, Wakayama: 'European Eye on Japan'
2004 – Museu de Arte de São Paulo, São Paulo: 'São Paulo'
2004 – Museo d'Arte Moderna e Contemporanea, Rovereto: 'Mimmo Jodice dalla collezione Cotroneo'
2005 – Galleria d'Arte Moderna, Bologna: 'Light'
2006 – Italian Institute of Culture, Tokyo: 'Mito Mediterraneo'
2006 – Castel Sant'Elmo, Naples: 'Campi Flegrei'
2006 – Galleria dell'Oca, Rome: 'Anima Urbis'
2006 – Palazzo Reale, Naples: 'Città visibili/Visible Cities'

# Selected Public Collections

University Art Museum, Albuquerque
Musée Reattu, Arles
Museum Photographic Archive, Barcelona
Detroit Institute of Modern Art, Detroit
Musée Cantini, Marseilles
Museo di Fotografia Contemporanea, Cinisello Balsamo–Milan
Galleria Civica d'Arte Moderna, Modena
Canadian Centre of Architecture, Montreal
Yale University Art Gallery, New Haven
Aperture Foundation, New York
Museo di Capodimonte, Naples
Bibliothèque Nationale de France, Paris
Maison Européenne de la Photographie, Paris
Fond National d'Art Contemporain, Paris
Philadelphia Museum of Art, Philadelphia
Centro Studi e Archivio della Comunicazione, Parma University
Istituto Nazionale per la Grafica/Calcografia, Rome
Museo d'Arte Contemporanea Castello di Rivoli, Turin
Museum of Modern Art, San Francisco
Fondazione Sandretto Re Rebaudengo, Turin
Galleria Civica d'Arte Moderna e Contemporanea, Turin
Museu de Arte de São Paulo, São Paulo
Museo d'Arte Moderna e Contemporanea, Rovereto
Massachusetts College of Art, Boston
Museum of Modern Art, Wakayama